Drawing Your Way through the Jewish Holidays

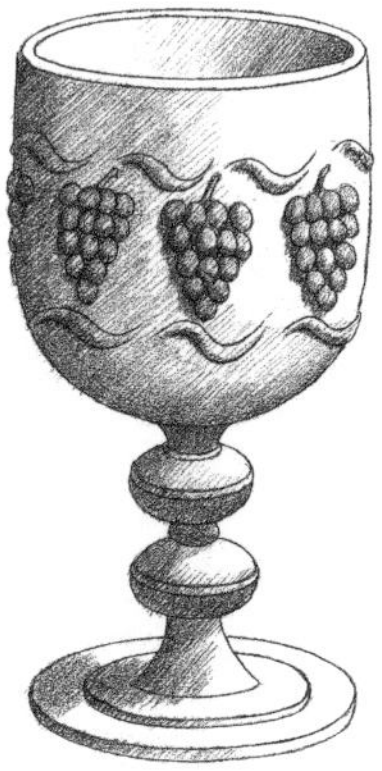

Written and Illustrated by

Eleanor Schick

UAHC Press
New York

For Sierra, Daniella, and Andrea

This book is printed on acid-free paper.

Manufactured in the United States of America
10 9 8 7 6 5 4 3 2 1

Preface

Drawing is a form of prayer. Through the use of pencil and paper, the artist in us communes with the physical and spiritual forces around us. For me, art is a way of expressing our wonder and admiration for the physical laws of the universe.

An object in space is defined by its edges; depth and texture are added by the way in which light falls upon the object. When I study an object's shape, weight, and texture, using my pencil to describe what I see, I experience a oneness with the world that cannot be expressed in words. Drawing the ritual objects of the Jewish tradition is an especially profound experience because my reverence for spatial forms responds to the sacredness of the objects I am drawing.

In this book you will learn how to look at an object with the eye of an artist and, using a few simple steps, re-create on paper the form of that object. What may first appear to be an intricately designed artifact resolves itself into a set of discrete simple objects. Thus a pair of Shabbat candlesticks is formed from a set of circles and ovals; a shofar emerges from a few simple curved lines; a spice box is generated from a group of rectangles and triangles.

When given the opportunity to express our appreciation for God's creations, we experience a deeply spiritual satisfaction. Like prayer, drawing offers such an opportunity. When we draw, we honor our Creator by re-creating the objects around us with our hands, our eyes, and our heart. Drawing is an act of reverence for the world around us and for the Creator of that world. Through *Drawing Your Way through the Jewish Holidays,* I hope you experience the same feeling of reverence that I do.

—Eleanor Schick

Begin lightly.

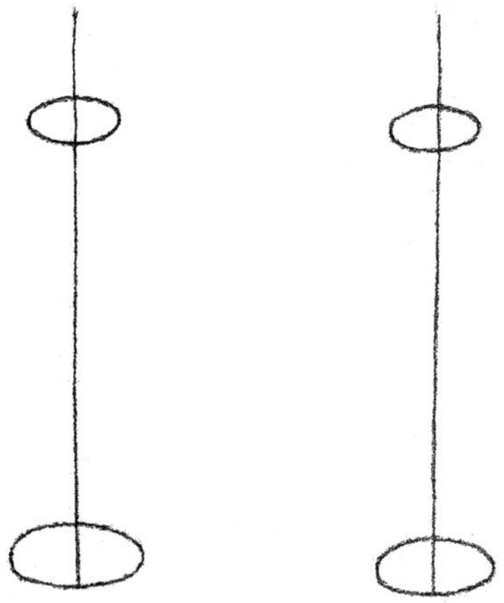

1. Begin with 2 lines. Add 2 horizontal ovals on each line, as shown, making the bottom ovals larger.

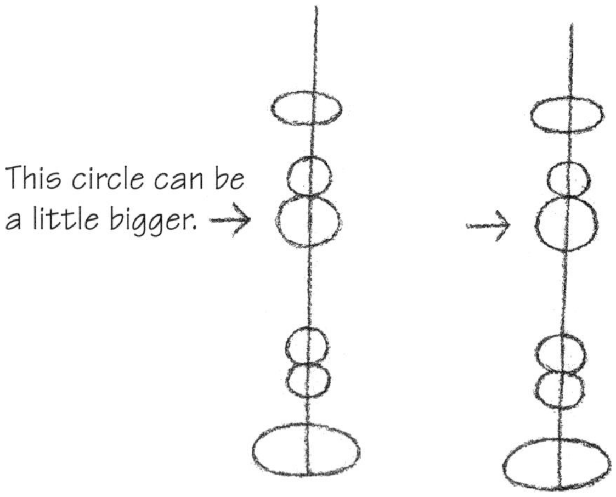

2. Add 4 circles on each line, as shown.

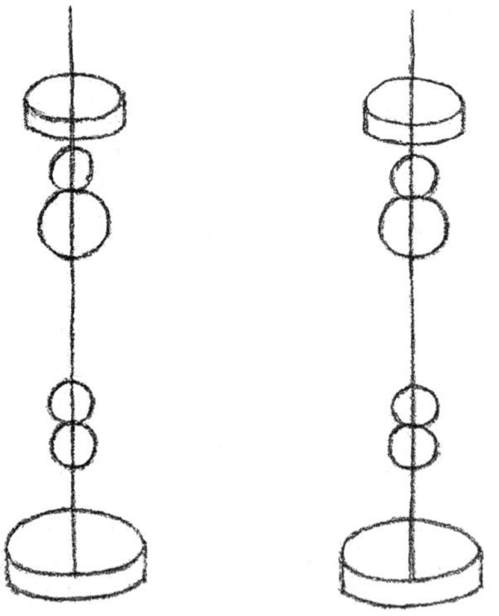

3. Double the line on the lower edge of each oval, as shown.

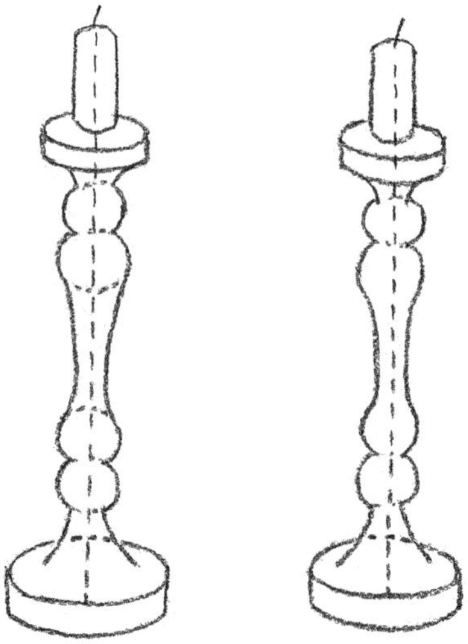

4. Shape the candlesticks and add the candles, as shown. Erase the dotted lines.

שַׁבָּת Shabbat

Shabbat is welcomed by lighting candles and reciting the blessing, "Blessed are You, the Eternal our God, Ruler of the universe, who makes us holy with mitzvot and commands us to kindle the lights of Shabbat."

נֵרֹת Candles

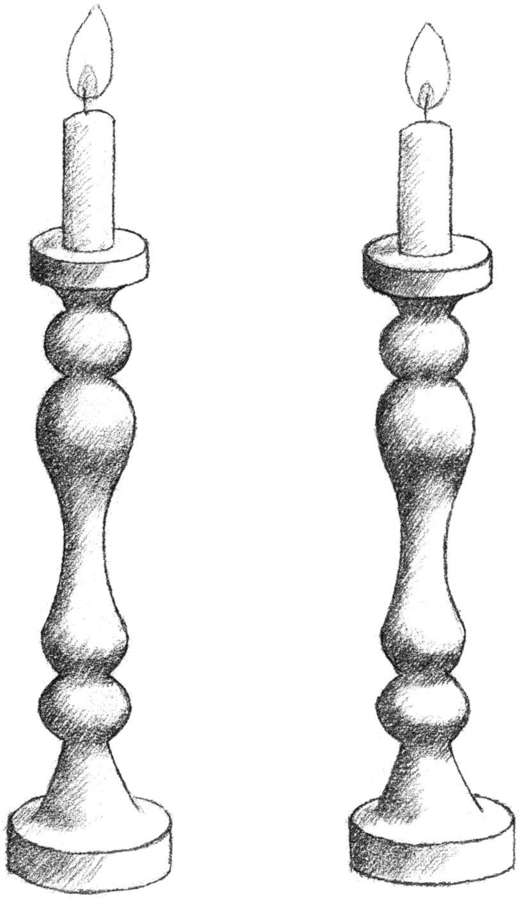

5. Darken your drawing. Add shadow.
   Draw flames on the candles.

All the beginning lines are guidelines, so start lightly.

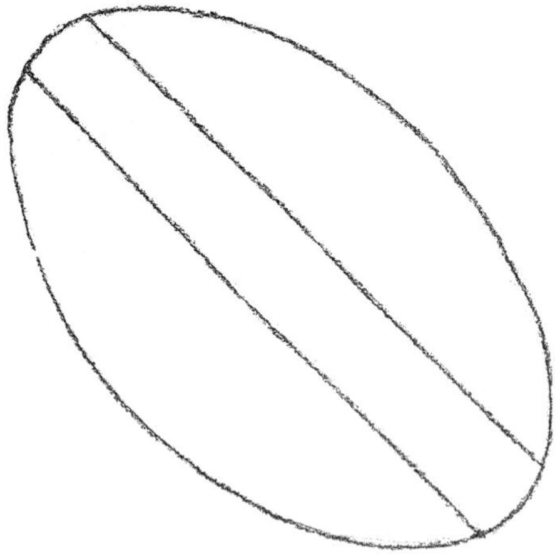

1. Draw a large oval with 2 lines down the center.

These shapes don't have to be even. Challah never comes out looking even.

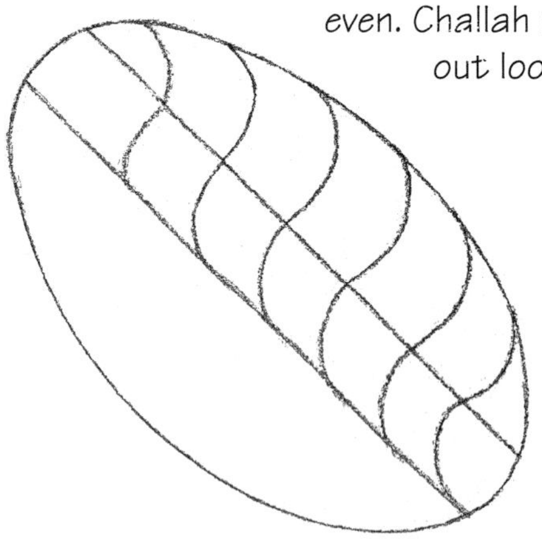

2. Make curving lines from the right side to the left center line.

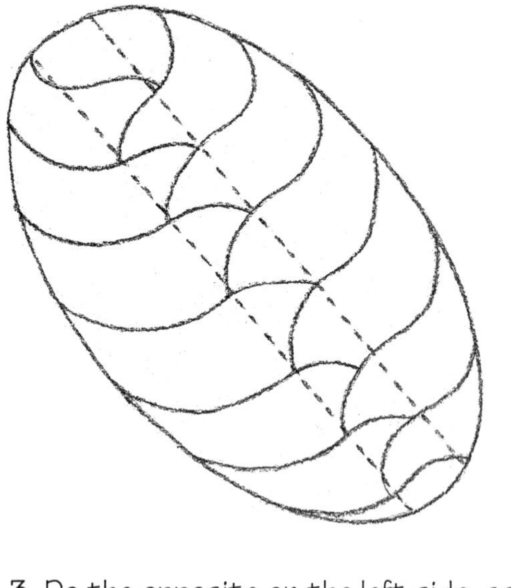

3. Do the opposite on the left side, as shown. Erase the dotted lines.

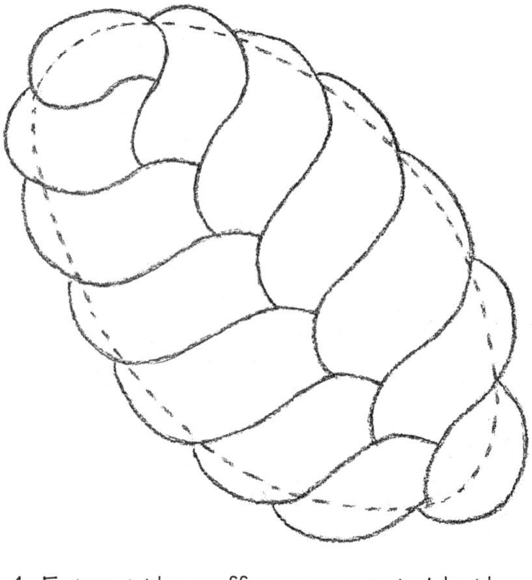

4. Extend the puffy curves outside the original oval. Erase the dotted lines.

שַׁבָּת Shabbat

Before the Shabbat meal begins, Jews lift the challah, a bread made specially for Shabbat, and recite the blessing, "Blessed are You, the Eternal our God, Ruler of the universe, who brings forth bread from the earth."

חַלָּה Challah

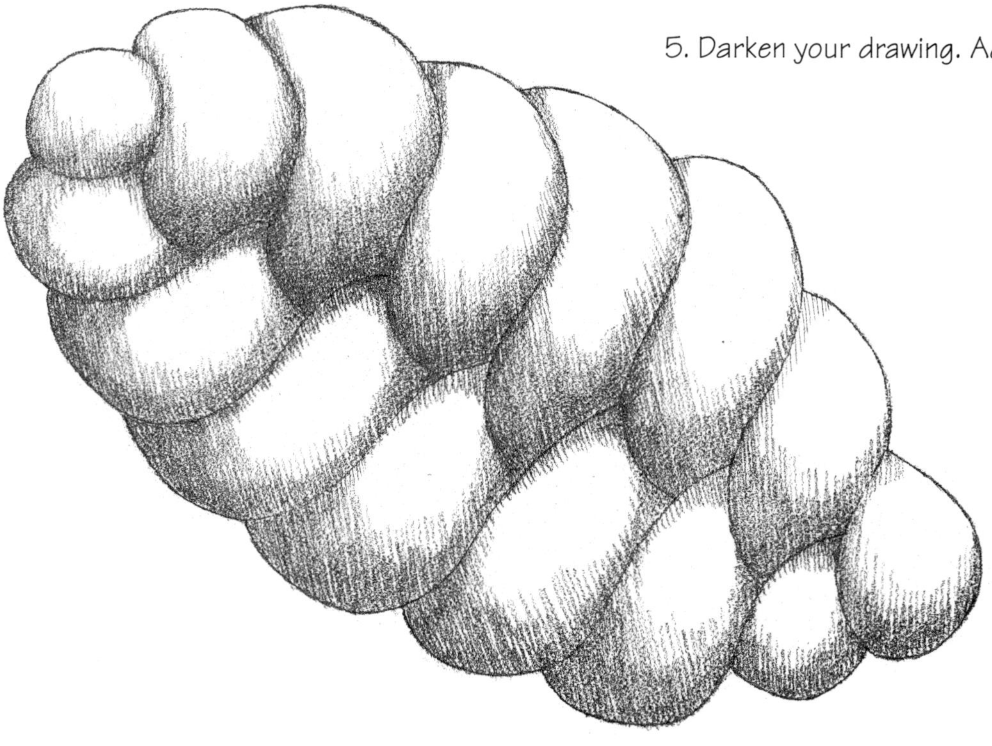

5. Darken your drawing. Add shadow.

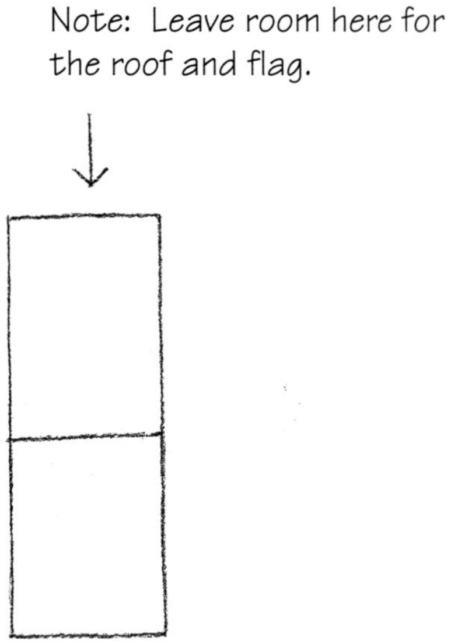

1. Draw a high rectangle with a line dividing it in half, as shown.

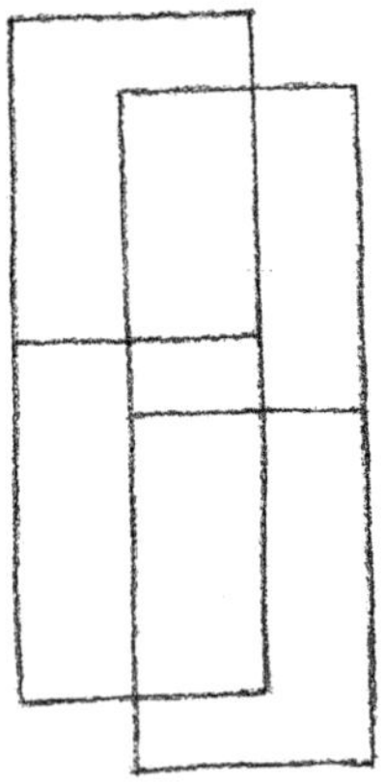

2. Draw another rectangle exactly like the first, as shown.

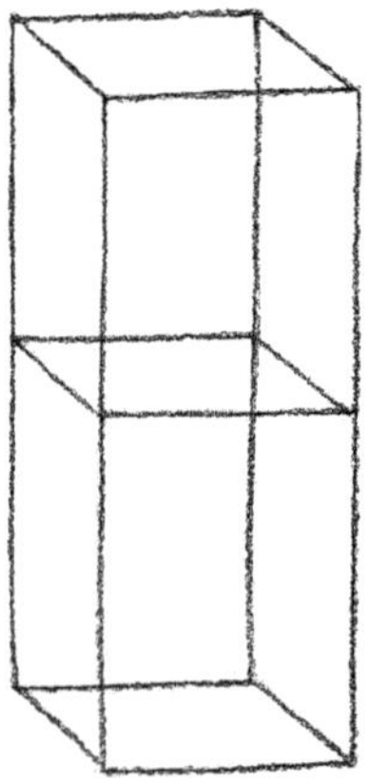

3. Connect the corners to make it 3-dimensional.

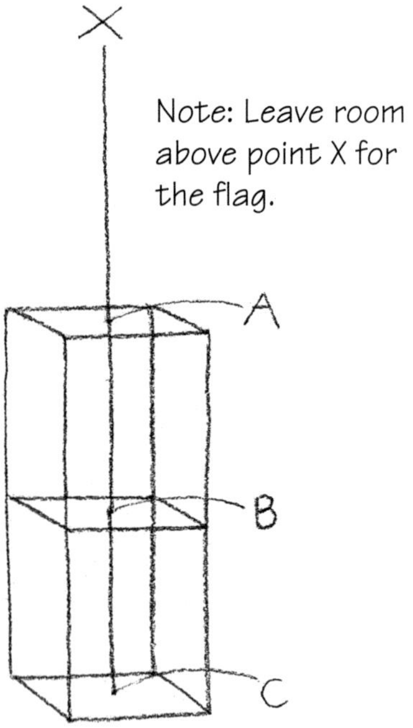

4. Mark the centers of sides A, B, and C. Draw a line through the centers all the way to point X.

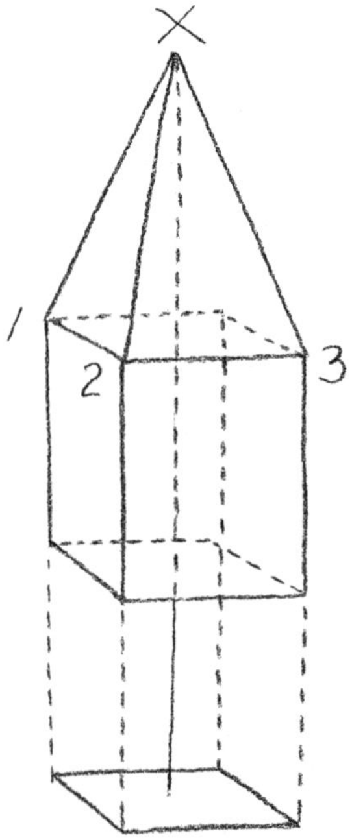

5. Connect corners 1, 2, and 3 to point X. Erase the dotted lines.

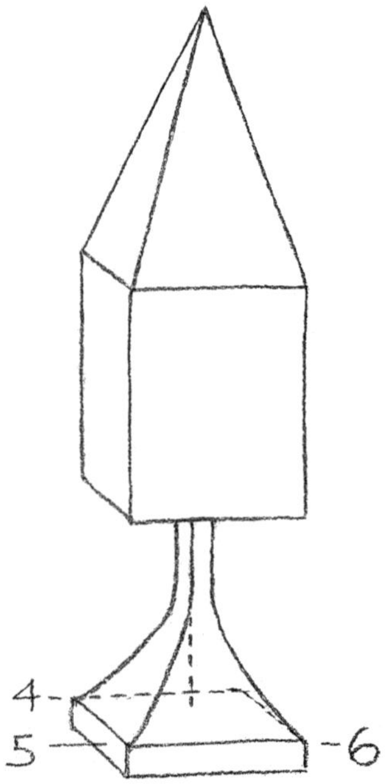

6. Shape the stand by arcing lines 4, 5, and 6, as shown. Thicken the base, as shown. Erase the dotted lines.

שַׁבָּת Shabbat

During the Havdalah ceremony, which marks the end of Shabbat, a blessing is recited before the sweet spices in the spice box are smelled: "Blessed are You, the Eternal our God, Ruler of the universe, Creator of all spices."

בֵּית תְּבָלִים Spice Box

Add a flagpole and a flag.

Add lines to decorate the roof.

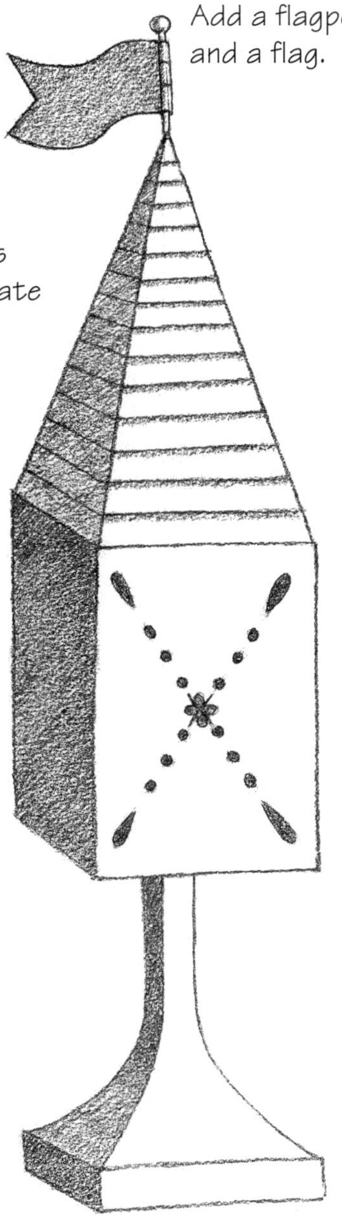

7. Darken your drawing. Make an X very lightly from corner to corner to make a decoration, and then erase the X. Add shadow.

Begin each drawing with guidelines. Guidelines are lines you will erase by the time your drawing is finished, so draw them very lightly.

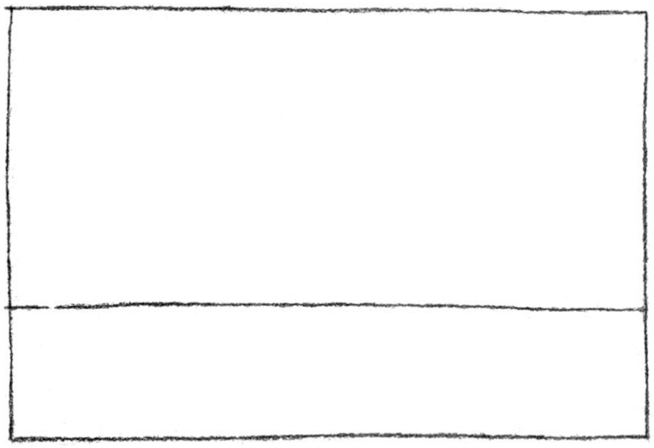

1. Begin with a rectangle. Draw a line across the bottom.

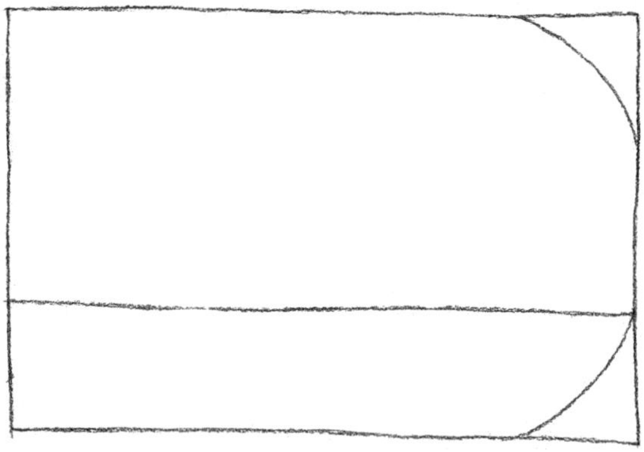

2. Add an arc in the upper and lower corners of the right side.

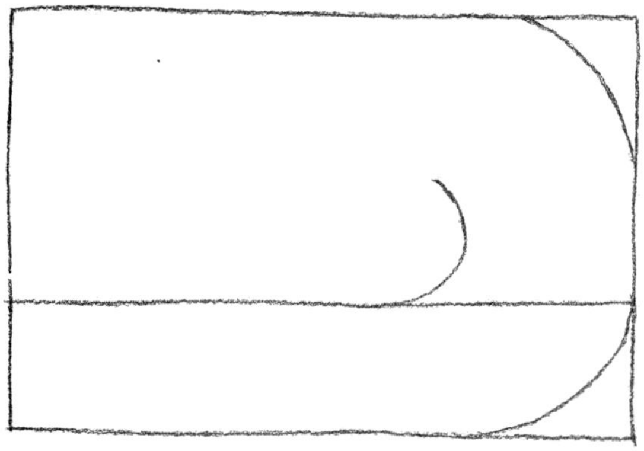

3. Add another small arc, as shown.

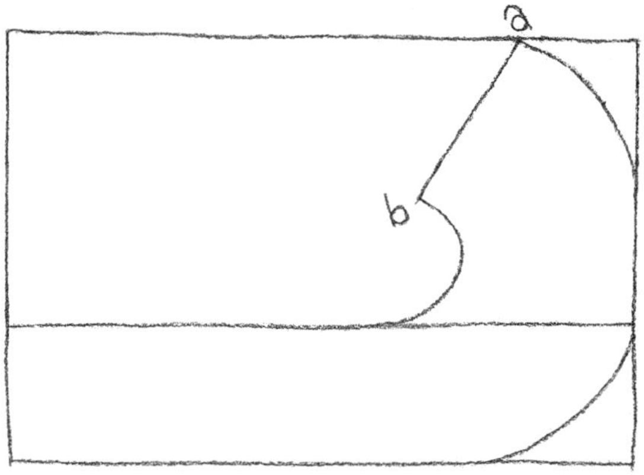

4. Draw a line from a to b.

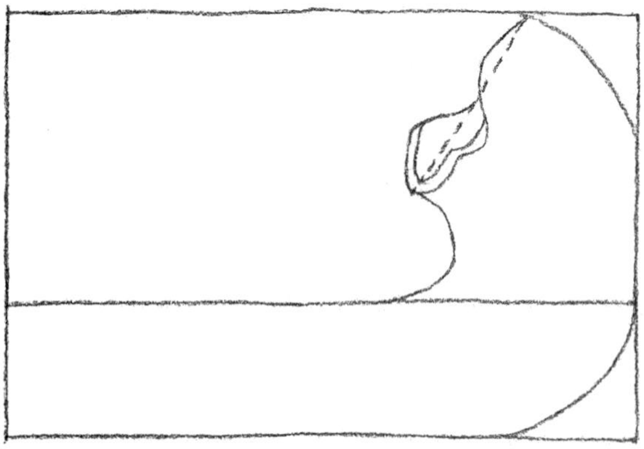

5. Shape the opening irregularly, as shown. Erase the dotted line.

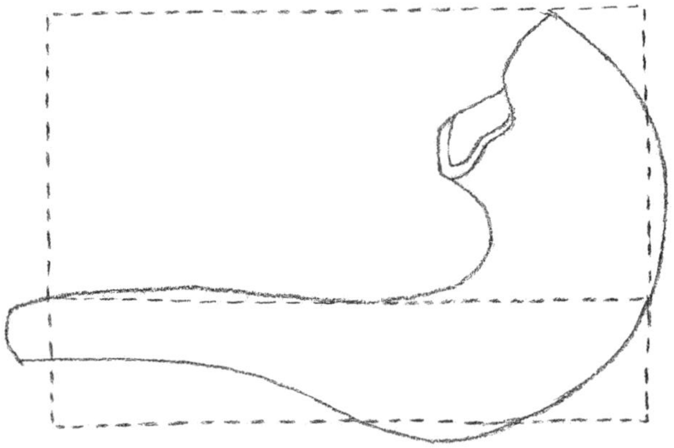

6. Shape the body of the shofar, as shown. Erase the dotted lines.

רֹאשׁ הַשָּׁנָה Rosh Hashanah

According to the great Jewish scholar Moses Maimonides, we blow the shofar on Rosh Hashanah, the Jewish New Year, to wake us up and remind us of God's existence and that we should do good.

שׁוֹפָר Shofar

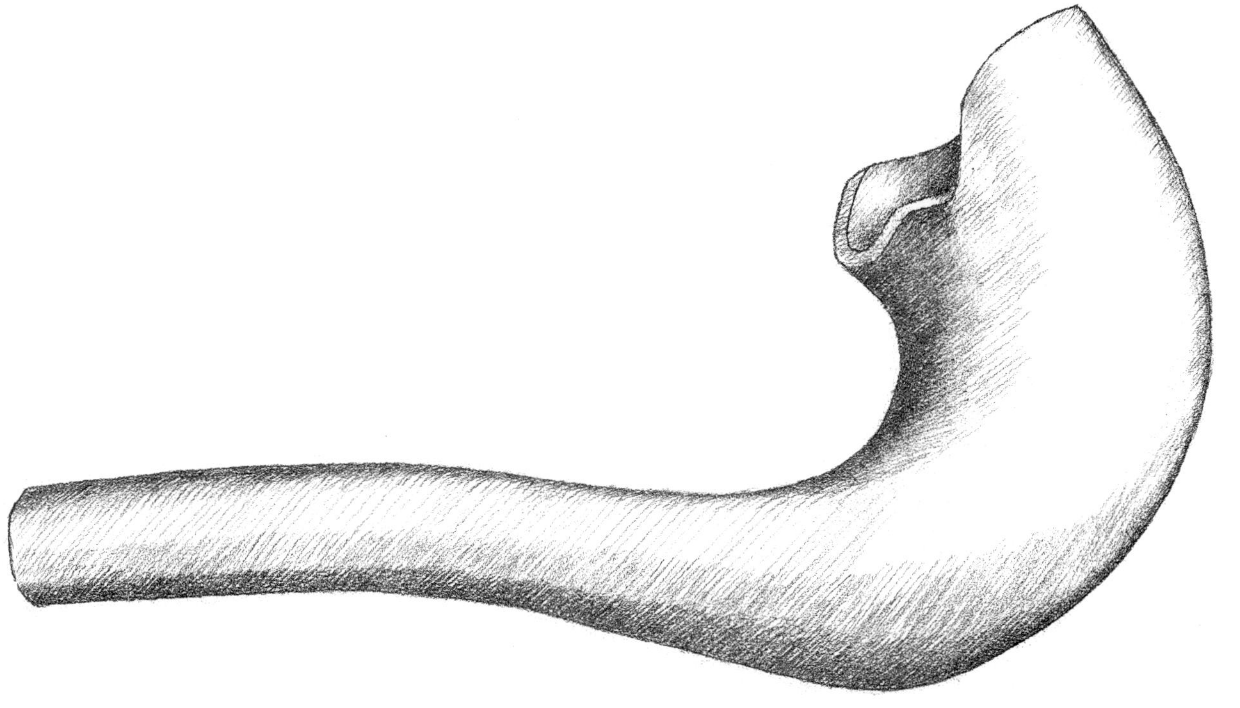

7. Darken your drawing. Add shadow.

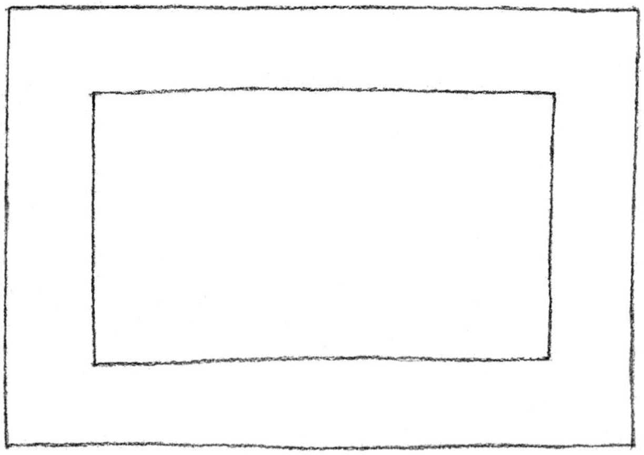

1. Begin with a rectangle and a smaller rectangle inside.

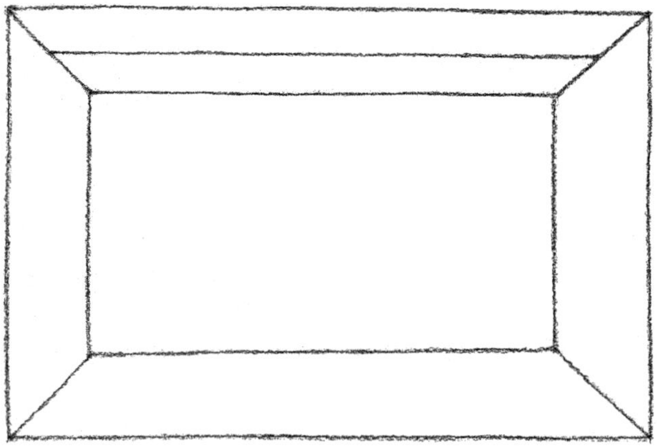

2. Connect the corners. Add a line across the top.

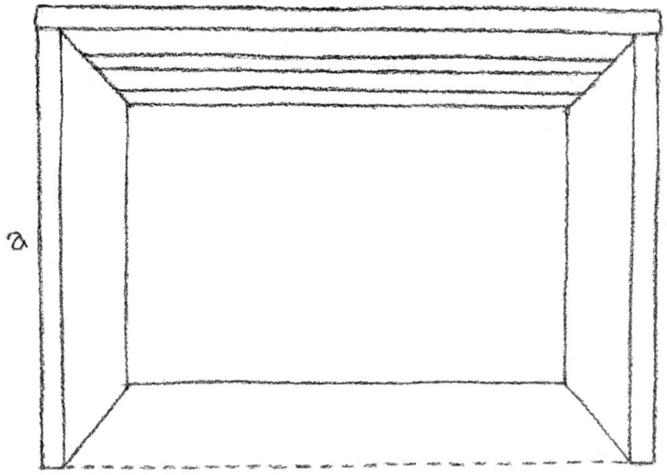

3. Double the lines across the top, as shown. These are your roof beams. Double the line for sides a and b. Erase the dotted line.

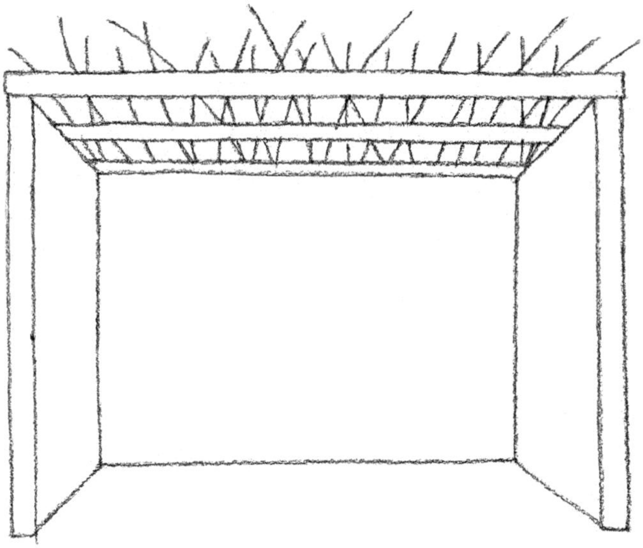

4. Add lines across the roof for branches. Erase where these lines go through the roof beams. Darken your drawing.

סֻכּוֹת Sukot

The sukah is an outdoor booth that we build for the holiday of Sukot, a time of great rejoicing. During the seven days we celebrate Sukot, we eat in the sukah and recall the ancient Israelites, who rested in such booths during the harvest season.

סֻכָּה Sukah

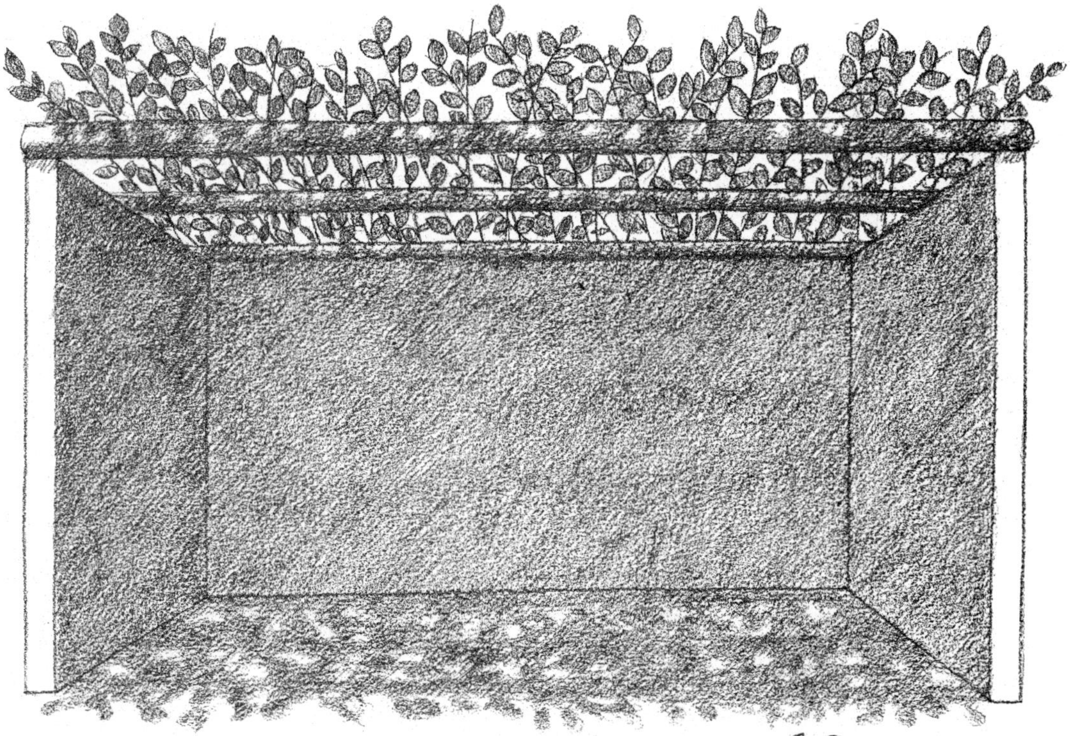

5. Put leaves on your branches. Mine are little ovals: 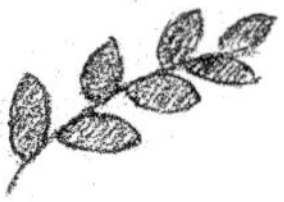
Add shadow.

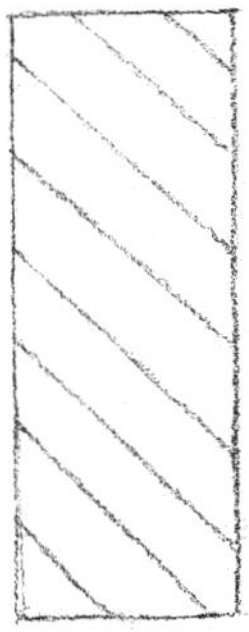

1. Begin with a very light upright rectangle for the trunk. Make some light diagonal lines across it.

2, Add spikes along the diagonal lines, as shown:

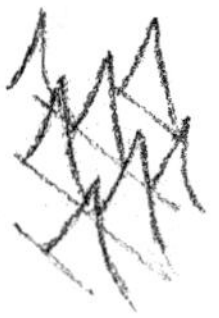

Add some spikes on the outer edges, too:

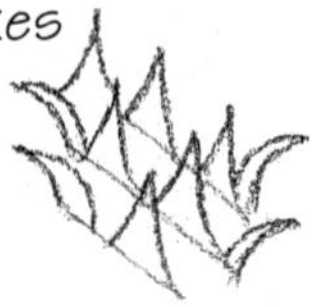

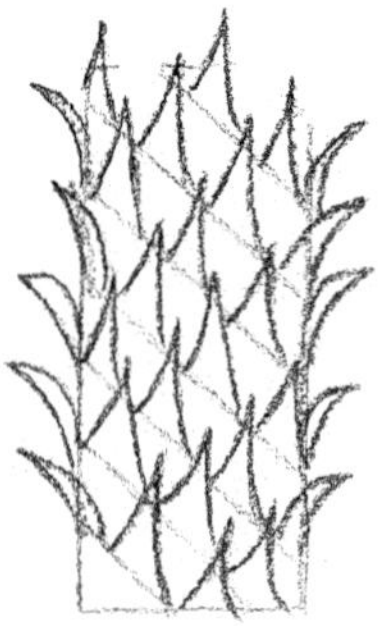

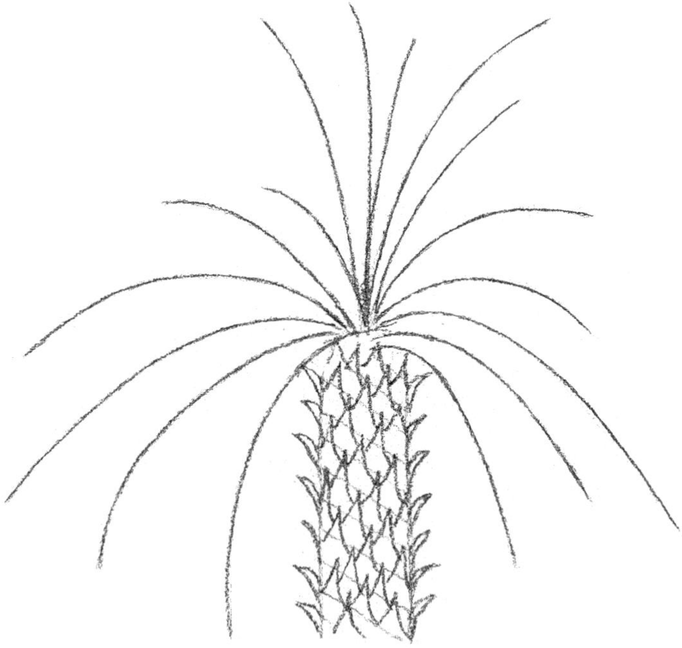

3. Add some long arcs coming from the top of the trunk for the branches.

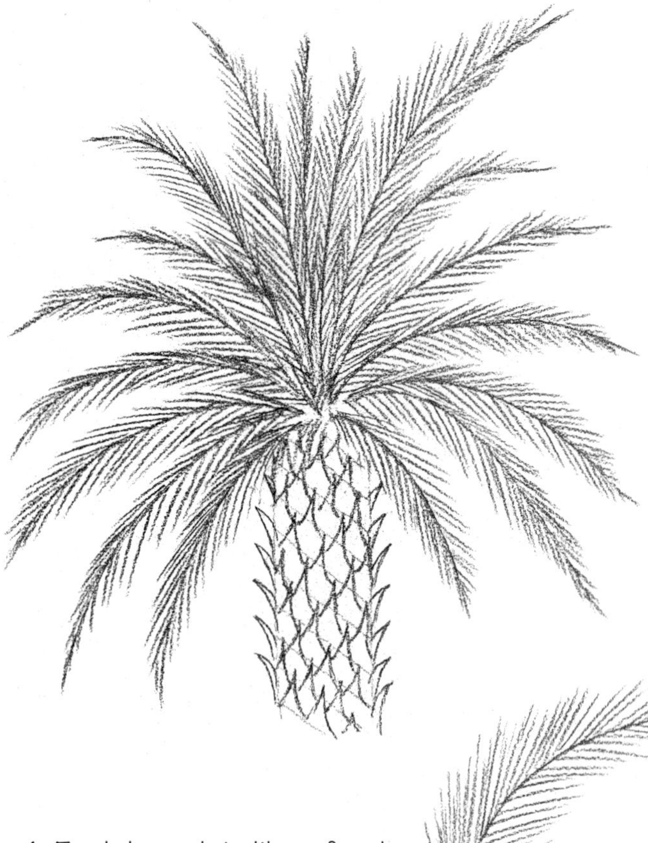

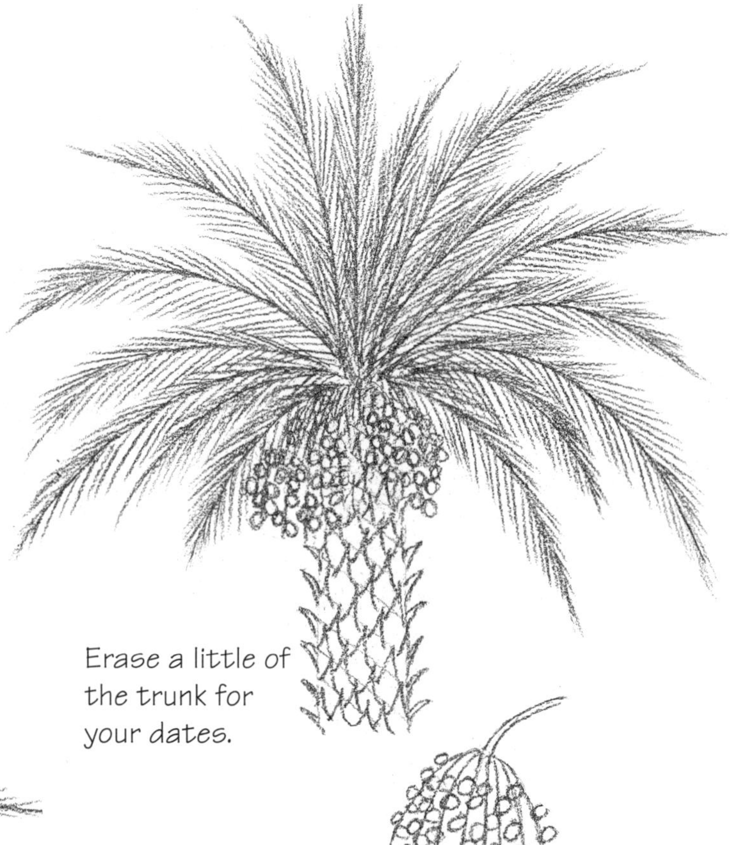

Erase a little of the trunk for your dates.

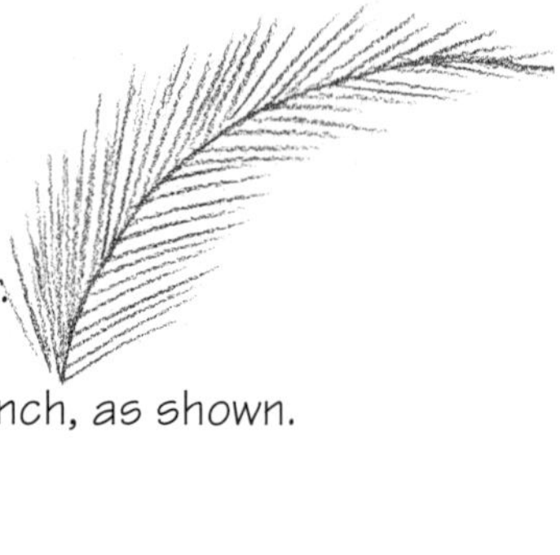

4. Each branch is like a feather. It tapers toward the tip: Draw the leaves on each branch, as shown.

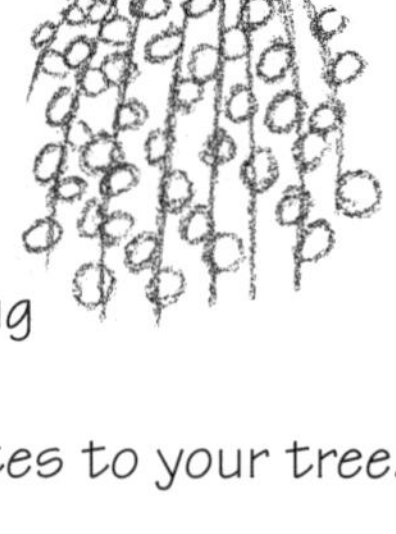

5. The dates hang in clusters: Add some dates to your tree.

סֻכּוֹת Sukot

On Sukot, Jews rejoice with a lulav, a young branch from a date palm that is attached to myrtle twigs and willow branches by a braided palm leaf. The lulav is waved in all directions to indicate that God is everywhere.

לוּלָב Lulav

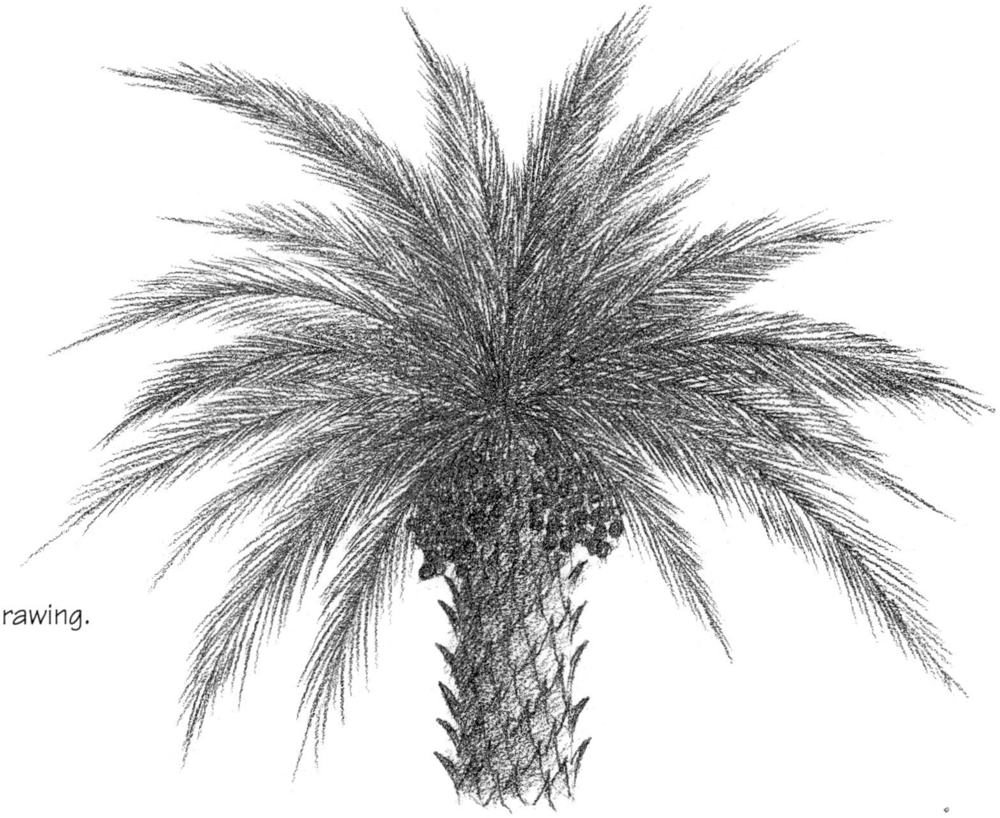

6. Darken your drawing.
   Add shadow.

Begin lightly.

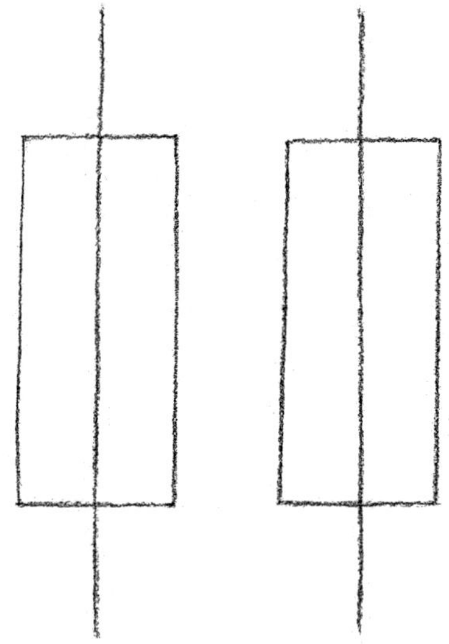

1. Begin with 2 rectangles. Draw a line through the center of each one.

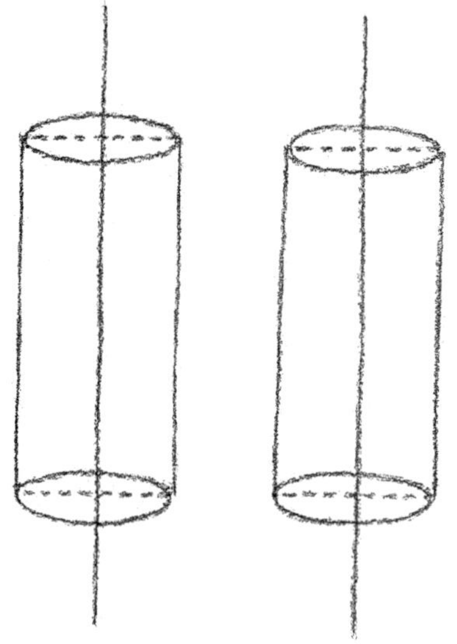

2. A horizontal oval at the top and bottom of each rectangle makes 2 cylinders. Erase the dotted lines.

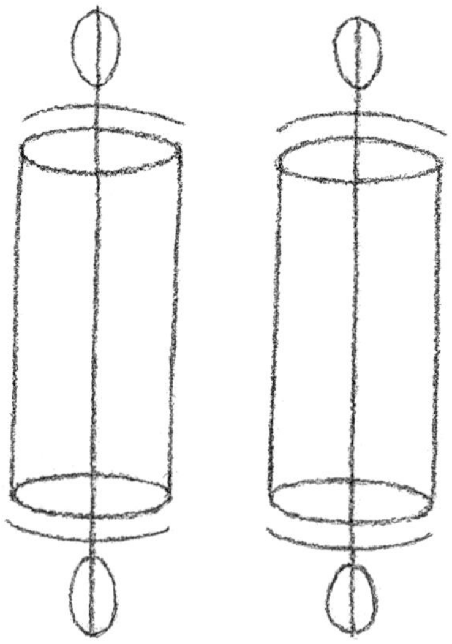

3. Double the outside line of each oval. Add an egg shape at the top and bottom of each center line.

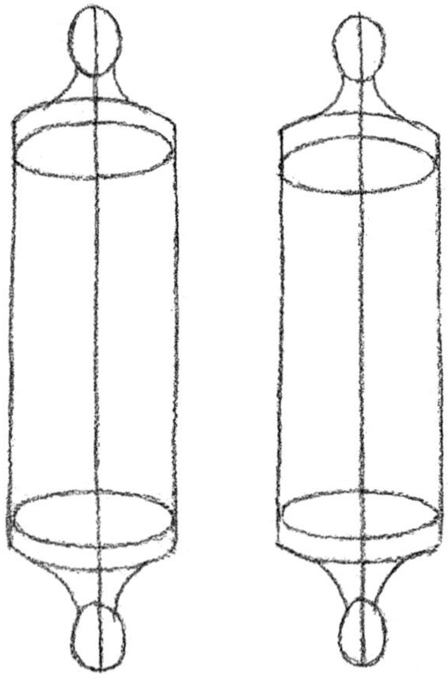

4. Shape the handles, as shown.

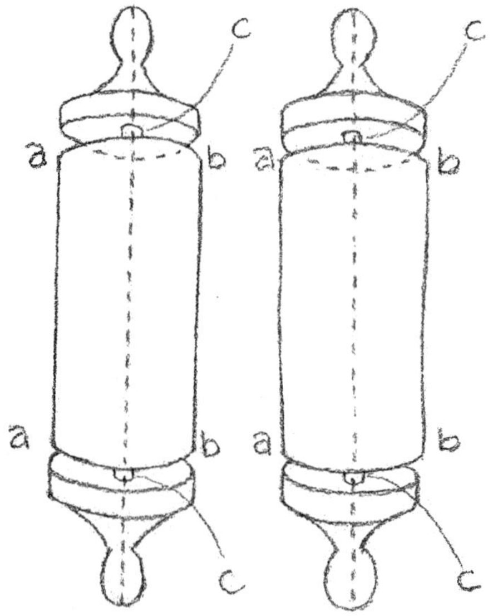

5. Draw in the scroll by making arcs from a to b, as shown. Indicate the centers (c) around which the scroll is rolled. Erase the dotted lines.

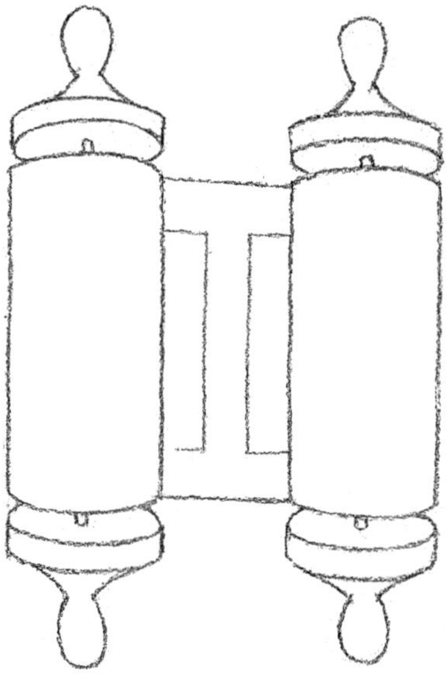

6. Make 2 horizontal lines showing the opened scroll. Very, very lightly, make guidelines for the text.

שִׂמְחַת תּוֹרָה Simchat Torah

The Torah, the Five Books of Moses, is read throughout the year in synagogues so that God's laws never cease to be read and heard. Jews end and begin the yearly cycle of readings on the same holiday, Simchat Torah.

תּוֹרָה Torah Scroll

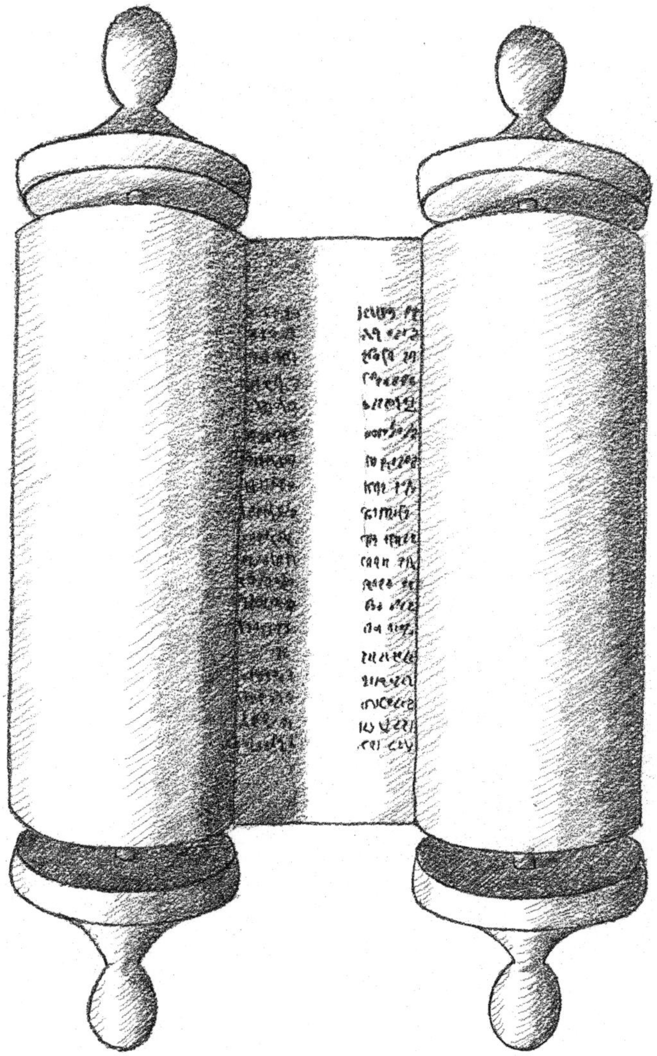

7. Darken your drawing. Show the text in the open part of the scroll. Add shadow.

Begin lightly.

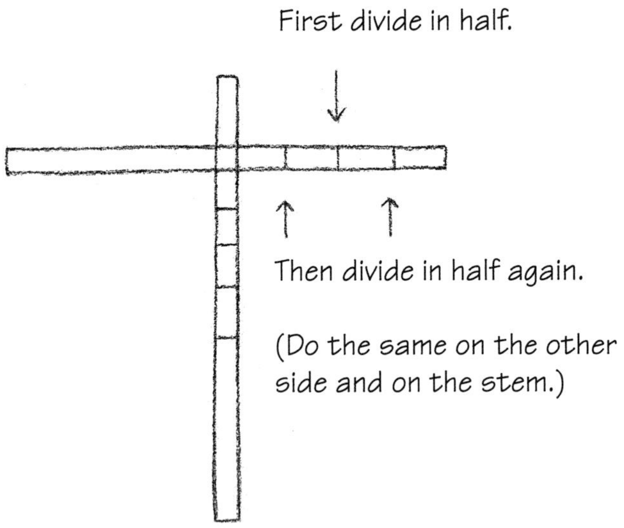

1. Draw 2 horizontal lines and 2 vertical lines. Mark 4 even spaces on each side of the horizontal bar and 4 even spaces on the vertical bar, as shown.

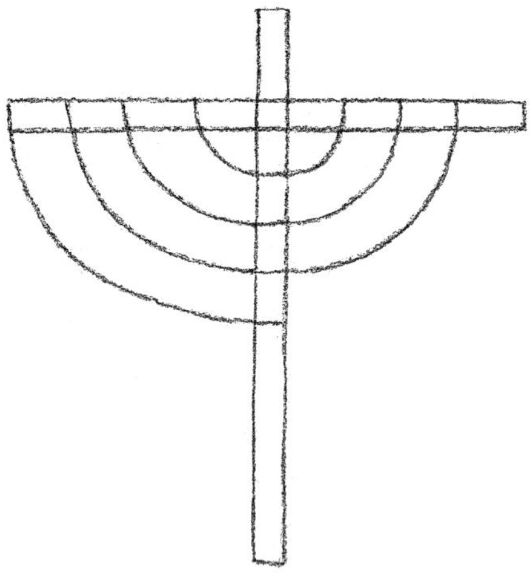

2. Draw arcs from each marker on the left through the center marker to the same one on the right side, as shown.

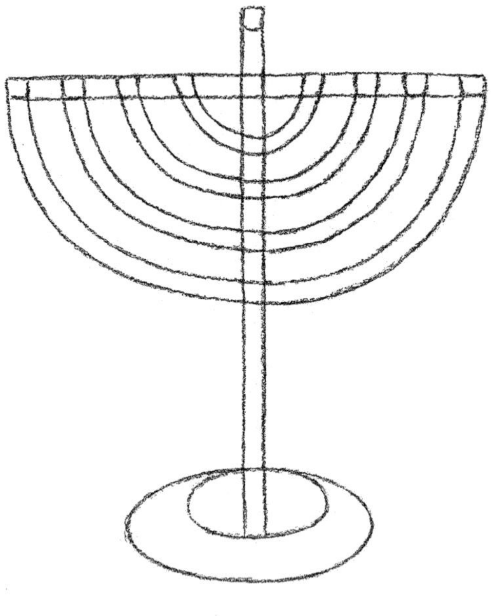

3. Double the arced lines. Add a cup for each candle and 2 ovals for the base. The ovals come together at the back.

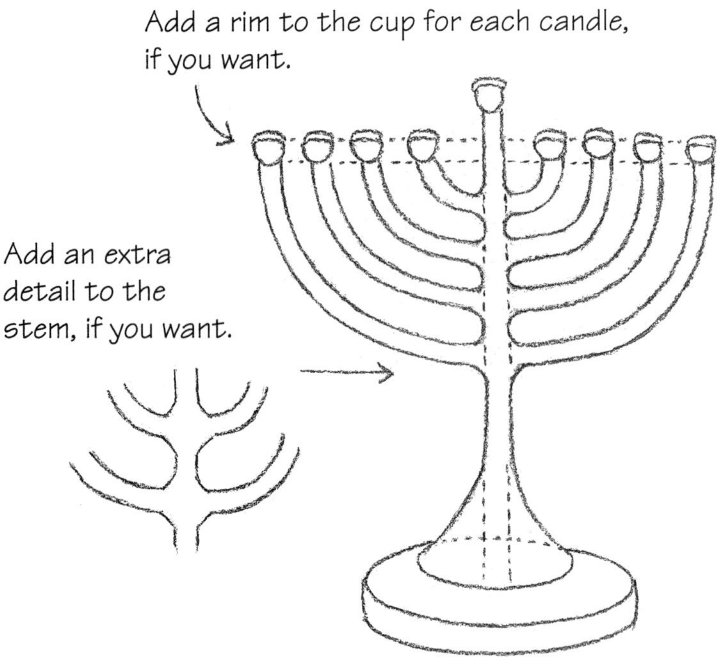

4. Shape the base. Erase the dotted lines.

חֲנֻכָּה Chanukah

The holiday of Chanukah is celebrated for eight days. According to Hillel, Jews add another candle to the Chanukah menorah each night in order to increase the holiness of the holiday.

חֲנֻכִּיָּה Chanukah Menorah

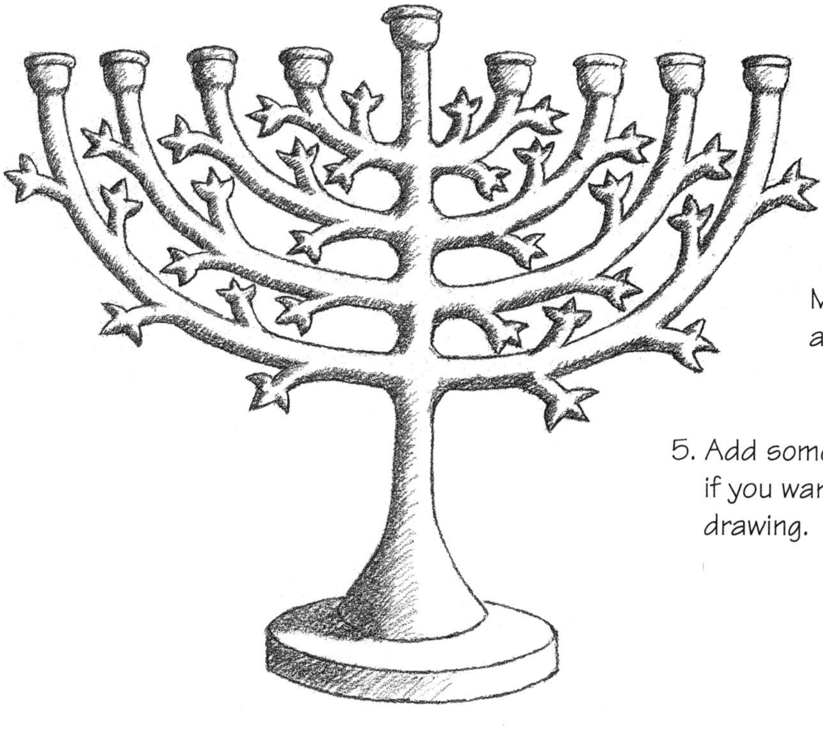

My decorations are 3 leaves: 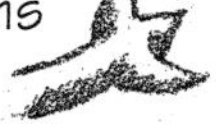

5. Add some decorations, if you want. Darken your drawing. Add shadow.

Begin lightly.

1. Begin with a square.

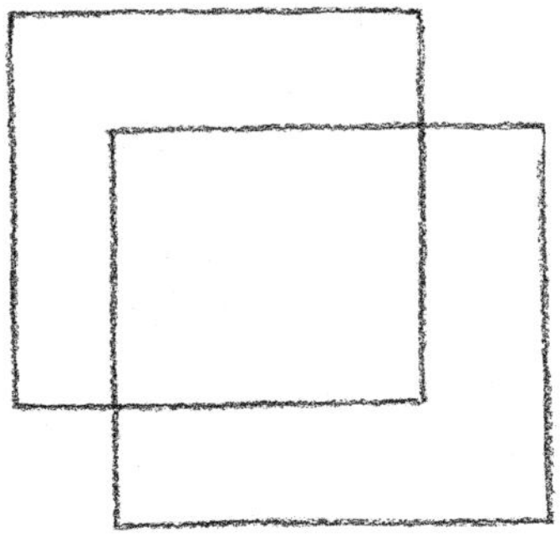

2. Add another square, as shown.

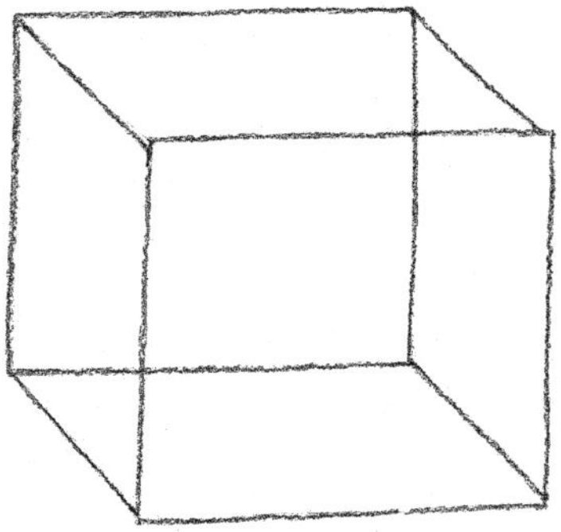

3. Connect the corners to make a cube.

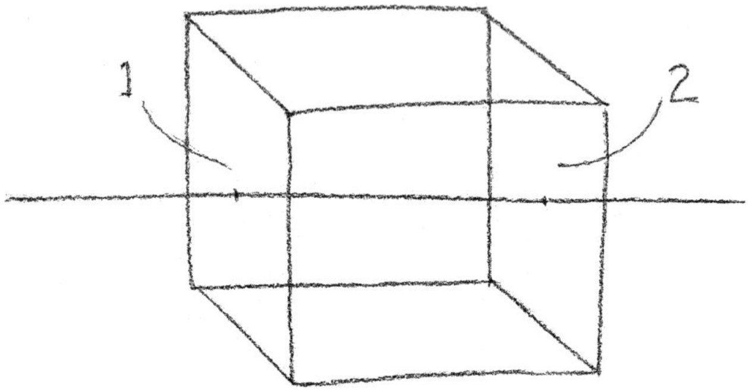

4. Mark the center of sides 1 and 2. Draw a straight line through the marks.

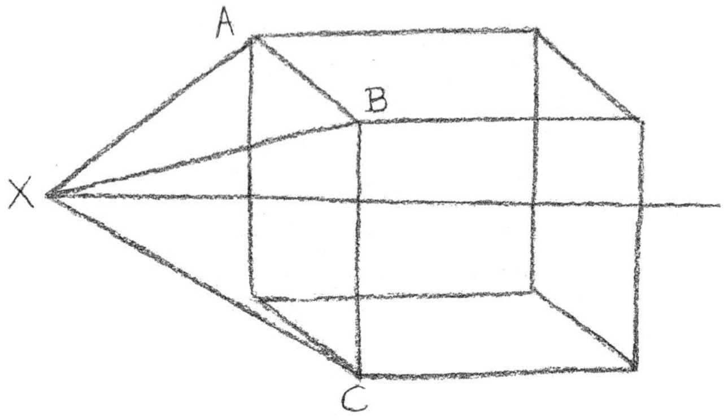

5. Draw lines from corners A, B, and C to point X.

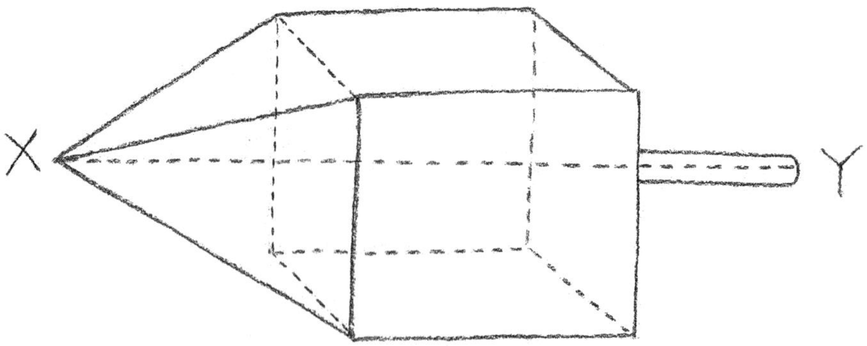

6. Make the line to point Y thicker, as shown. Erase the dotted lines. Darken your drawing.

חֲנֻכָּה Chanukah

One way we celebrate Chanukah is by spinning a four-sided top called a dreidel. On each side is a Hebrew letter. Together the four Hebrew letters stand for "A Great Miracle Happened There."

דריידל Dreidel

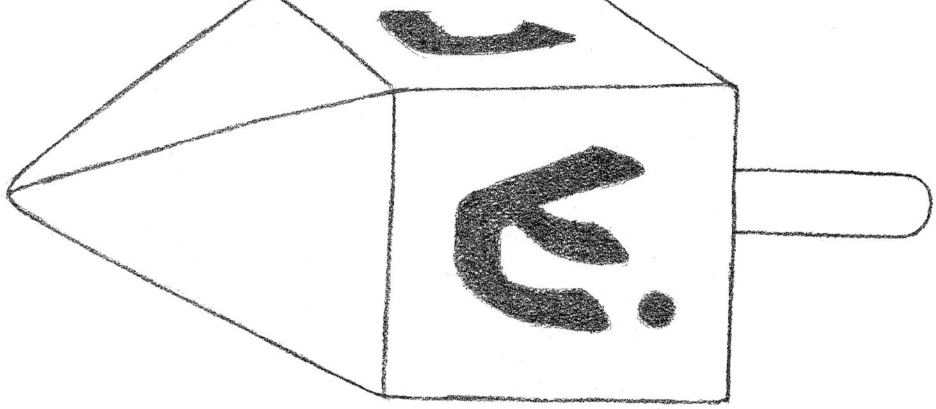

7. Turn the page sideways to draw the Hebrew letters.

Begin lightly.

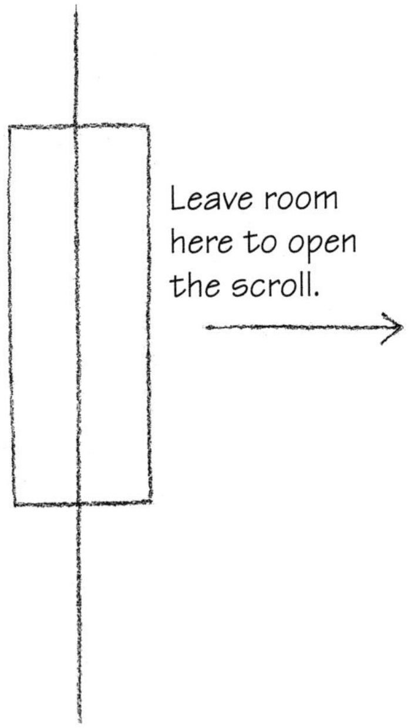

1. Draw an upright rectangle with a line down the middle.

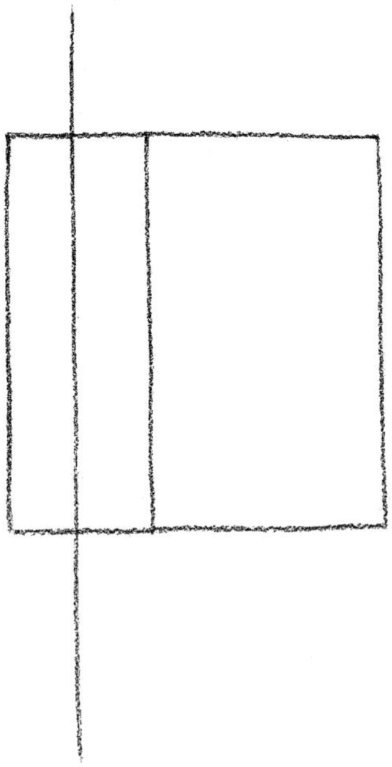

2. Add a wider rectangle by extending the horizontal lines to one side.

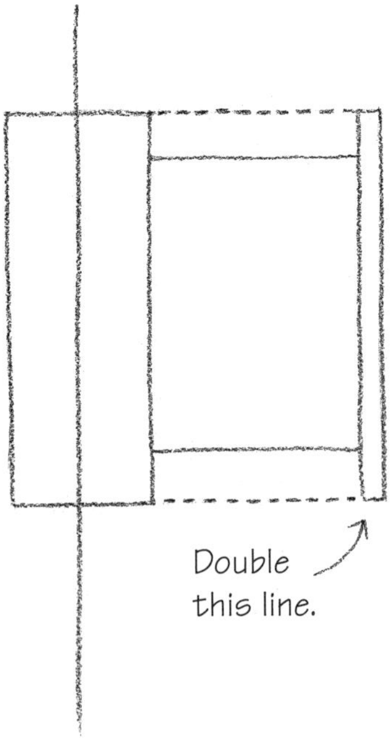

3. Modify the second rectangle, as shown. Erase the dotted lines.

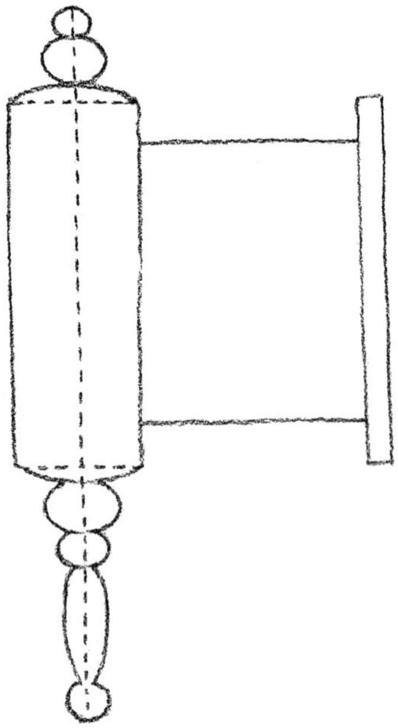

4. Add circles and ovals, as shown, to shape the handle of the scroll. Erase the dotted lines.

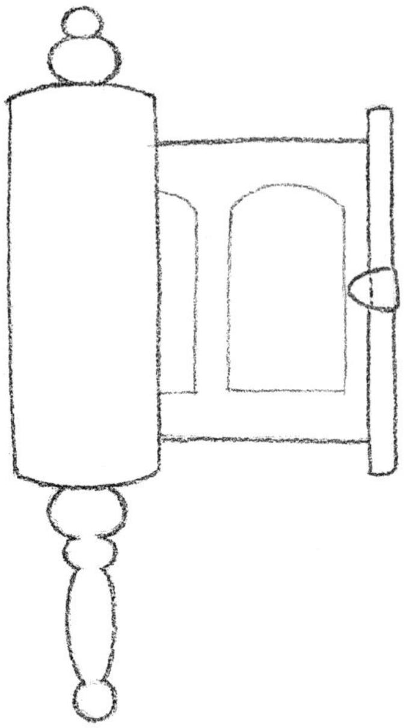

5. Very lightly, make shapes to outline the text of the scroll. Add a latch. Erase the dotted lines.

פּוּרִים Purim

The Megillah or Scroll of Esther is read on Purim, a holiday that celebrates Jewish survival. The entire scroll is read on the holiday of Purim.

מְגִלַּת אֶסְתֵּר Scroll of Esther

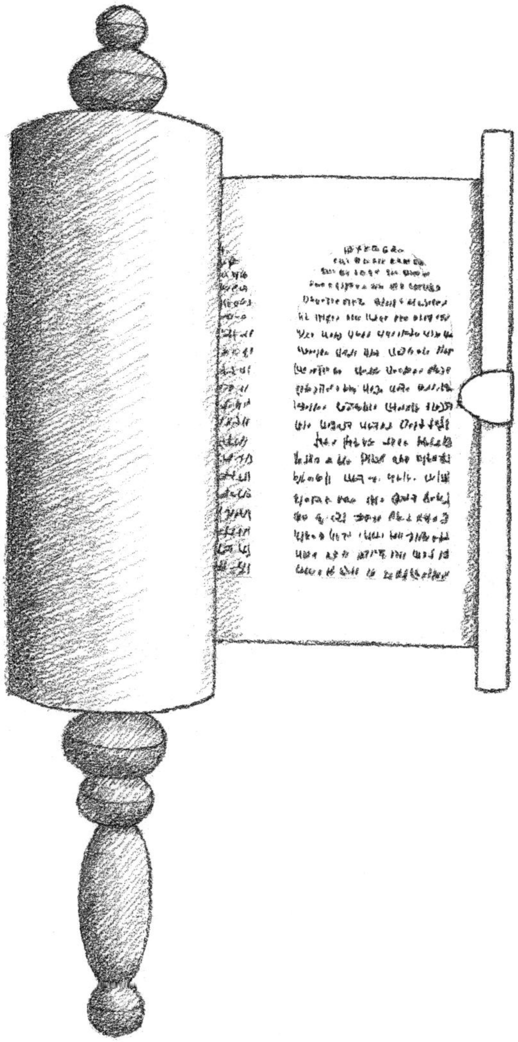

6. Add text to your scroll. Darken your drawing. Add shadow.

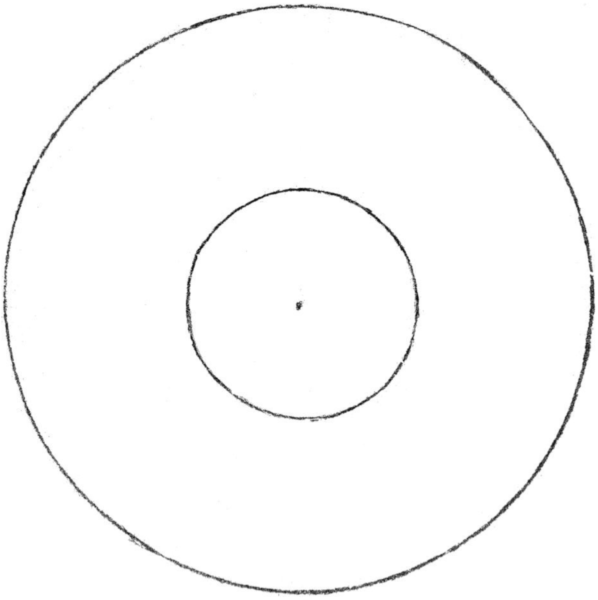

1. Begin with a circle.* Mark the center and make a smaller circle around it.

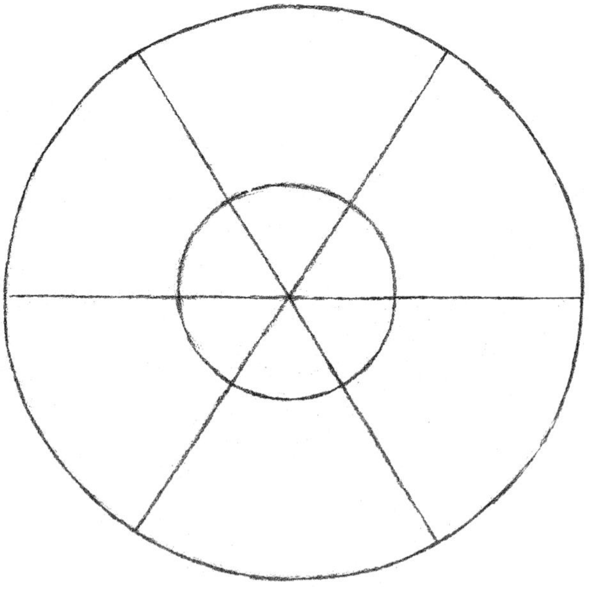

2. Divide the circle into 6 parts. Make a horizontal line through the center, then an X going through the center. These lines should be light.

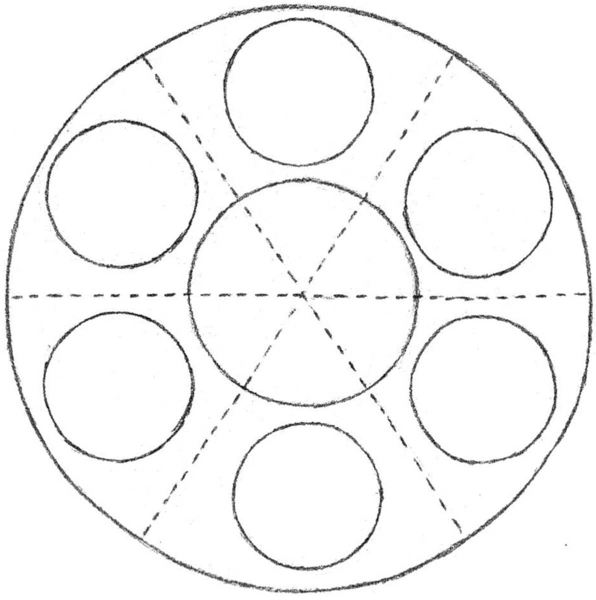

3. Draw a circle in each of the 6 sections. Erase the dotted lines.

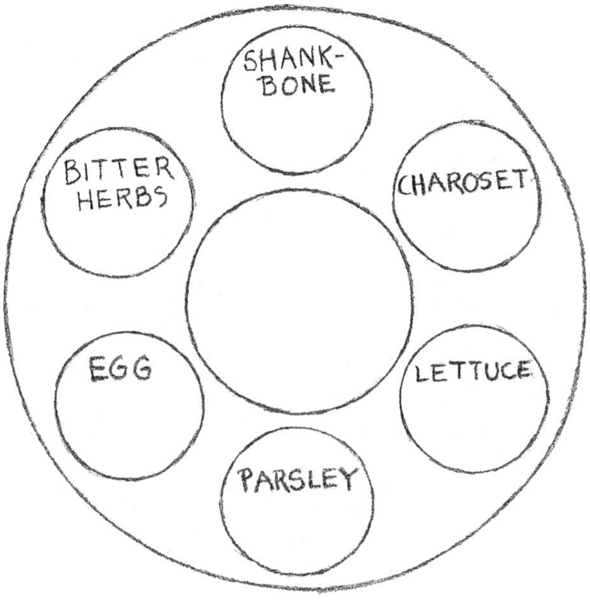

4. Write in the names of the special seder foods. Note: You may want to leave room to illustrate each one.

*Note: To get an even circle, trace a jar top or another circular object.

פֶּסַח Passover

nged on a special plate called the story of the Israelites' slavery and from Egypt.

Seder Plate

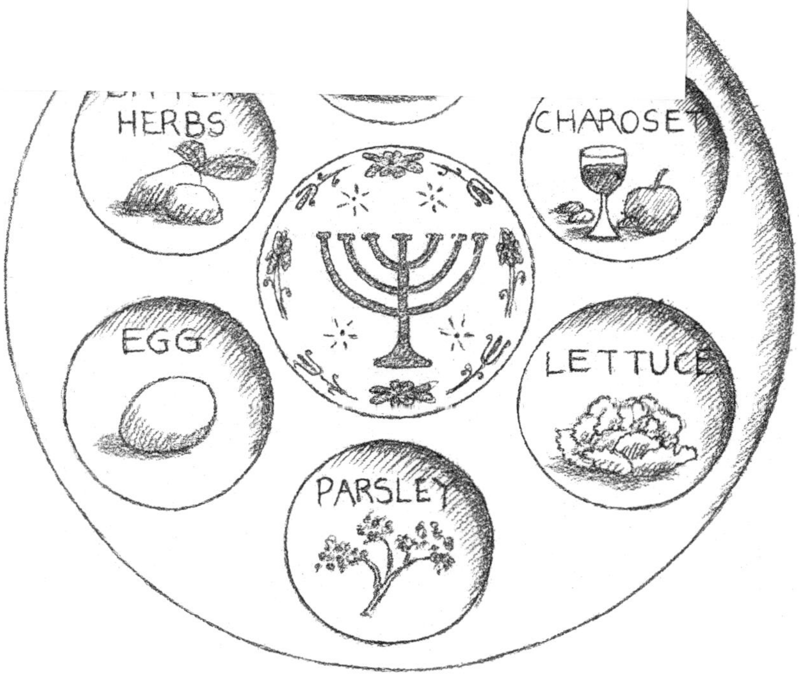

You can illustrate the seder foods on each section of the plate.

5. Draw a design in the center. Darken your drawing. Add shadow, if you want.

Begin lightly.

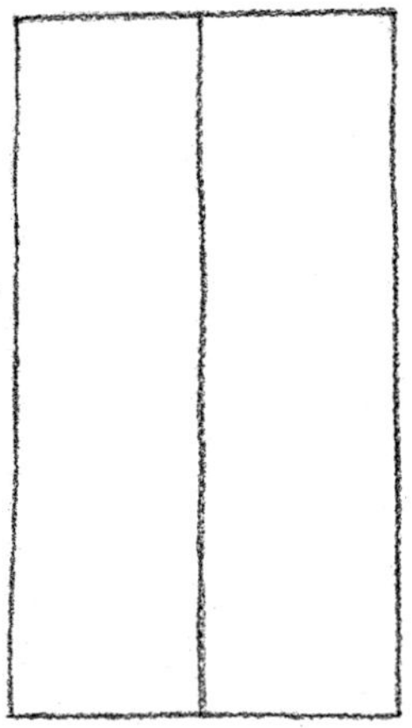

1. Draw a rectangle with a line down the center.

2. Draw ovals at the top and bottom to make a cylinder. Erase the dotted lines.

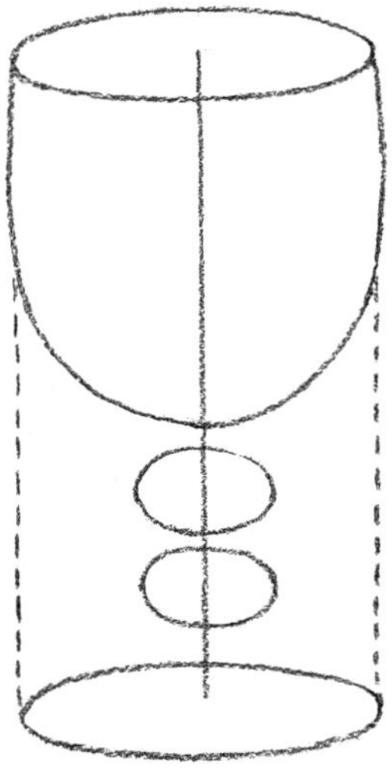

3. Draw an arc to shape the cup. Add 2 ovals on the stem. Erase the dotted lines.

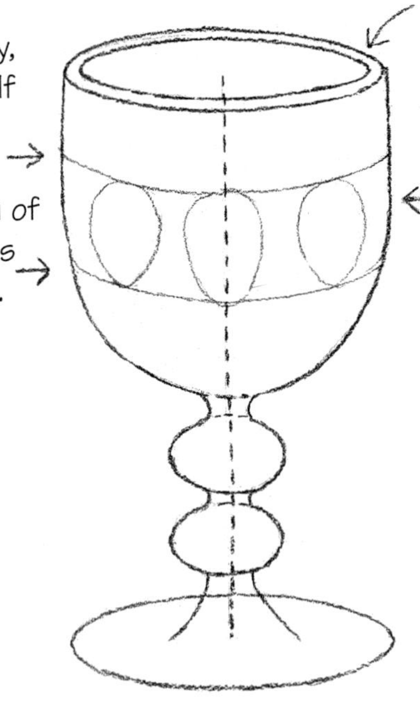

4. Shape the stem, as shown. Erase the dotted lines.

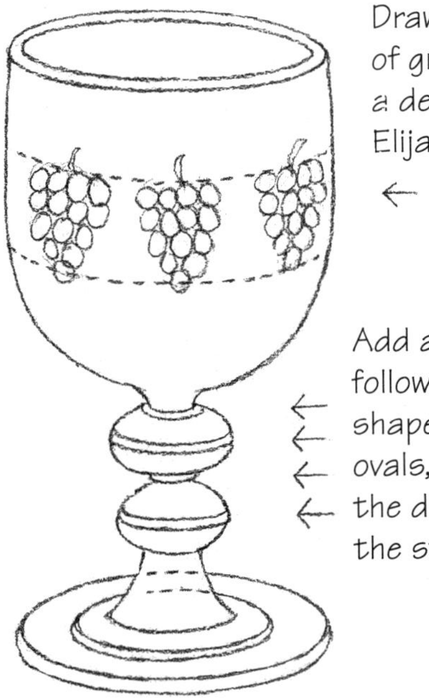

5. Add ovals for the base, as shown. Erase all the dotted lines.

פֶּסַח Passover

Passover is a holiday that celebrates freedom. During the Passover seder, a cup is placed on the table for the prophet Elijah, who Jews believe will announce the coming of the Messiah.

כּוֹס אֵלִיָּהוּ Elijah's Cup

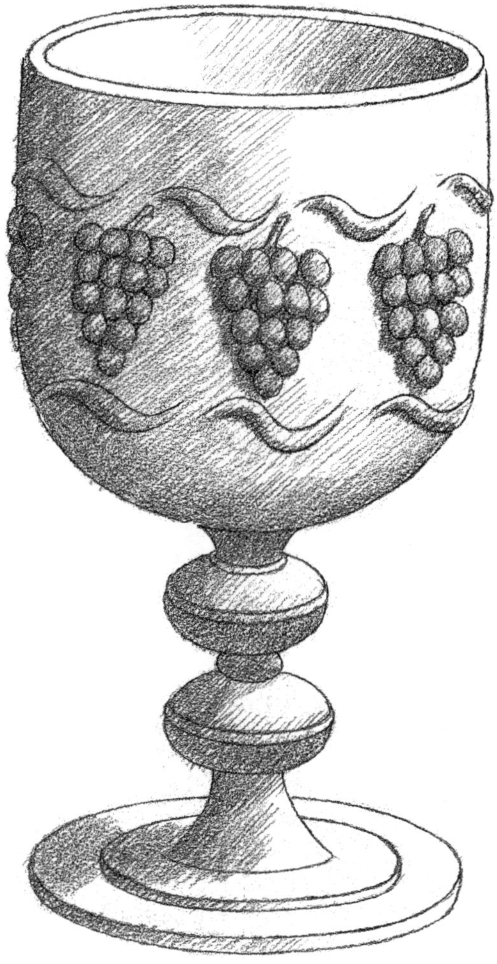

6. Darken your drawing. Add shadow. Add to the designs, if you want.

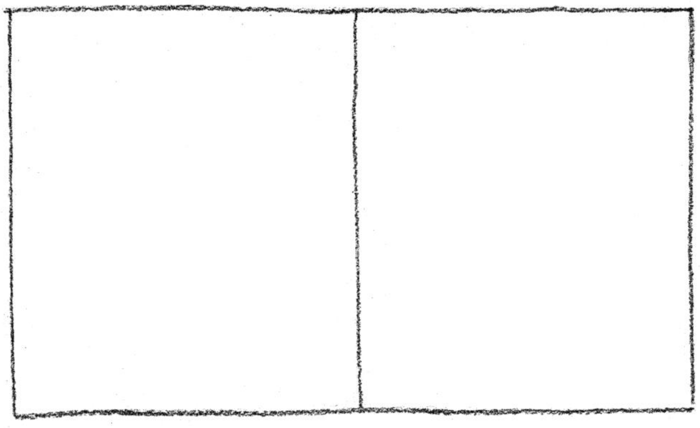

1. Begin with a rectangle. Very lightly, draw a vertical line down the center.

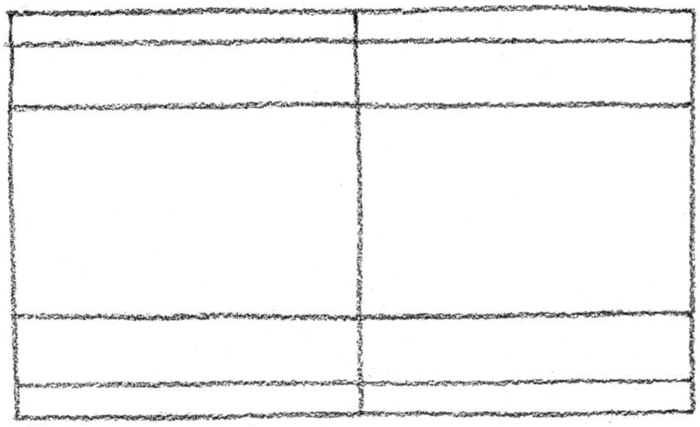

2. Draw 2 lines across the top and 2 lines across the bottom, as shown.

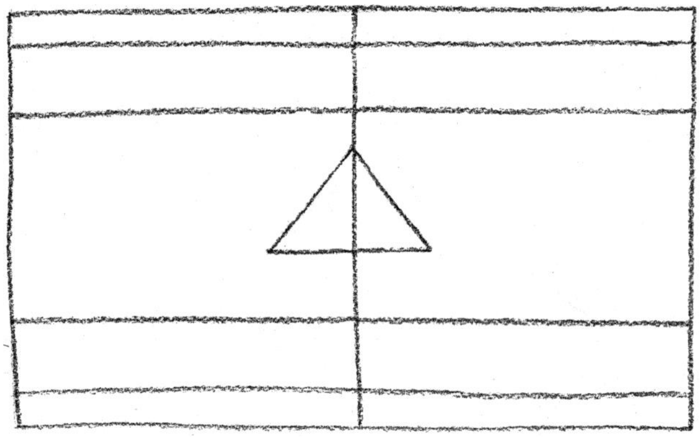

3. Draw a triangle with its point on the center line.

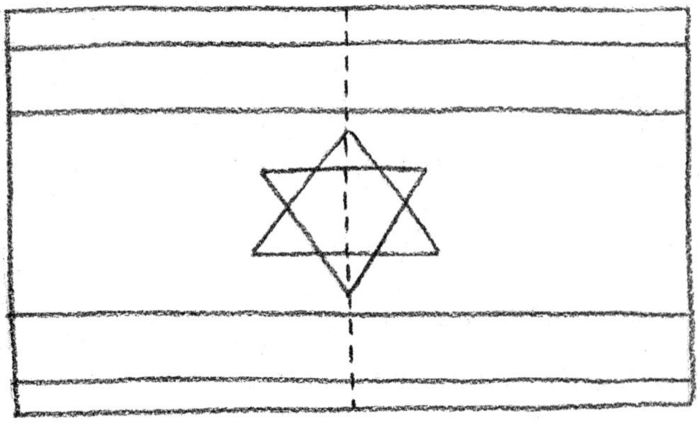

4. Draw an upside-down triangle with its point also on the center line. Erase the dotted line. Now you have a Star of David.

יוֹם הָעַצְמָאוּת Israel Independence Day

On Yom Ha'atzmaut, Israel Independence Day, Jews celebrate the founding of the State of Israel. The two stripes on the blue and white flag of Israel remind Jews of the traditional prayer shawl or talit.

דֶגֶל Flag

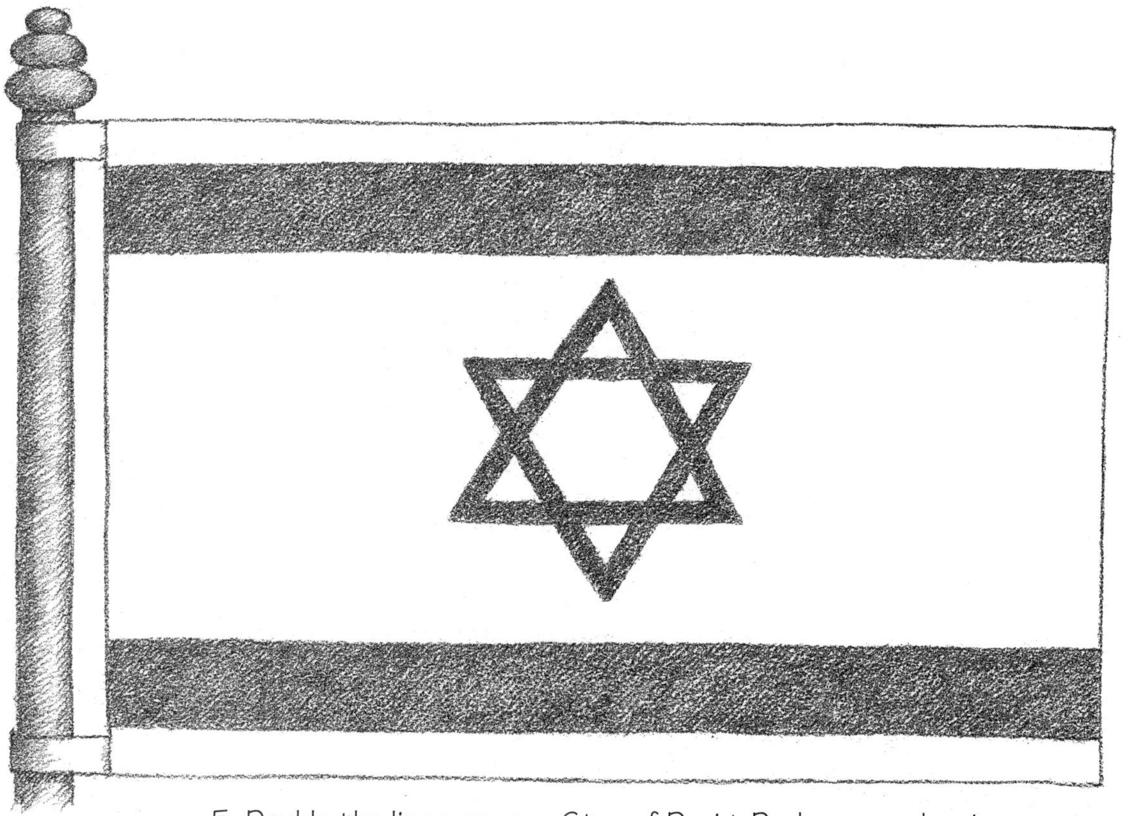

5. Double the lines on your Star of David. Darken your drawing. Shadow the star and the stripes. Add a flagpole, if you want.

Begin lightly.

1. Begin with an upright rectangle.

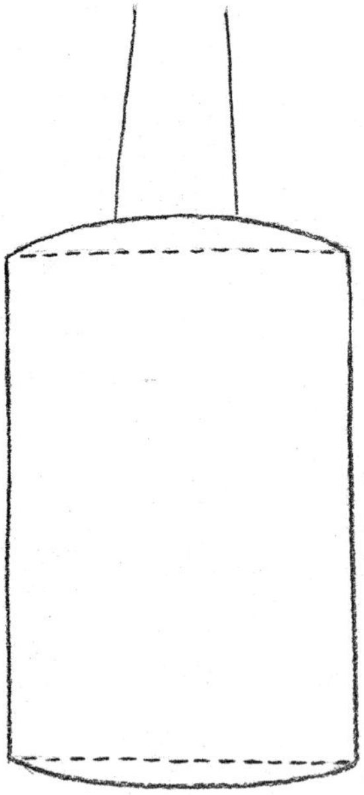

2. Round the lines on the top and bottom. Erase the dotted lines. Add 2 lines extending from the top.

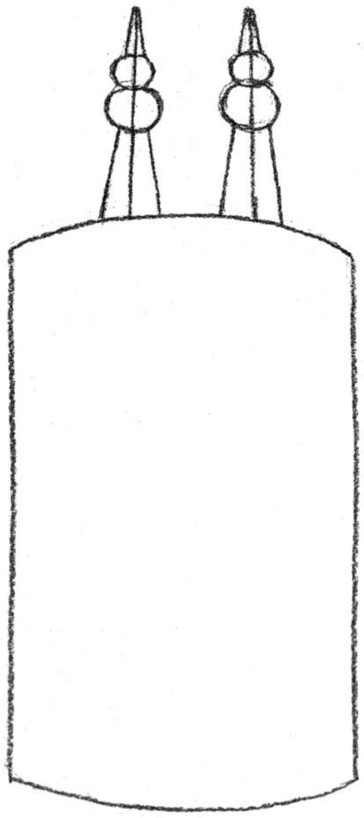

3.Make some shapes out of which you will design the finials, as shown.

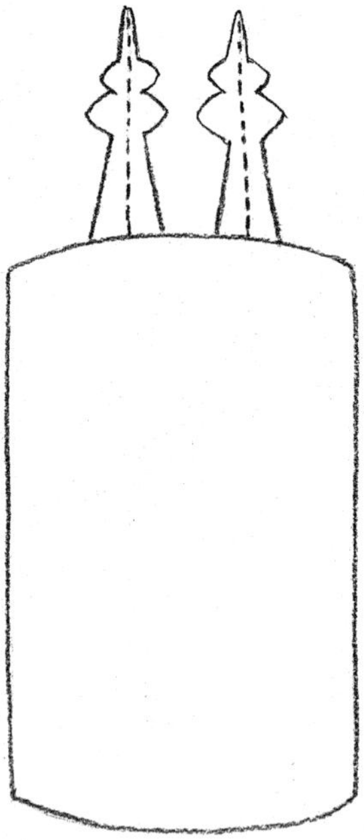

4.Shape the finials. Erase the dotted lines.

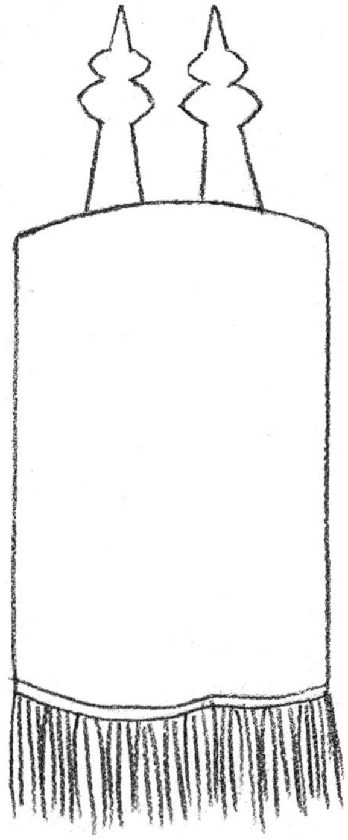

5. Add a fringe.

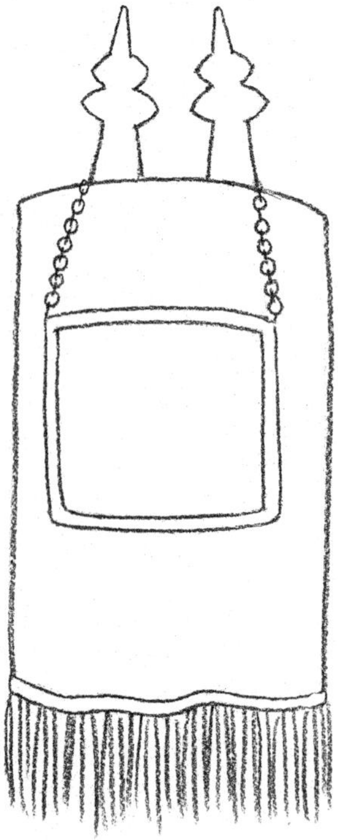

6. Add a breastplate and the chain it hangs from:

שָׁבוּעוֹת Shavuot

On Shavuot we celebrate God's gift of the Torah to the Jewish people. We recognize the majesty of the Torah by dressing it in a cover made of fine material, with decorative finials on top and an elaborately designed breastplate in front.

סֵפֶר תּוֹרָה Covered Torah Scroll

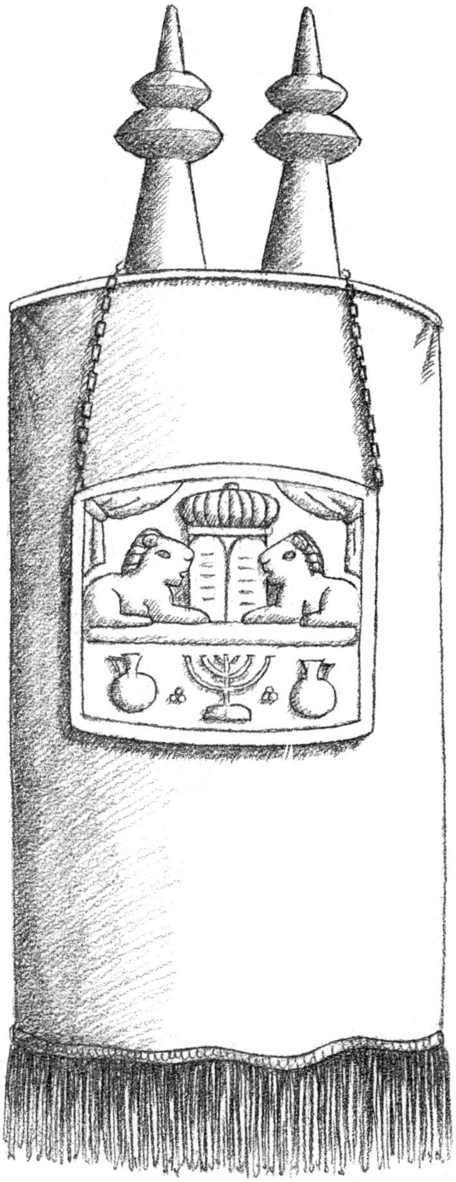

7. Darken your drawing. Make any design you want on your breastplate. Add shadow.